Steve Jobs

Computer Visionary

By Sophie Washburne

Portions of this book originally appeared in
Steve Jobs by Barbara Sheen

LUCENT
PRESS

Published in 2017 by
Lucent Press, an Imprint of Greenhaven Publishing, LLC
353 3rd Avenue
Suite 255
New York, NY 10010

Designer: Deanna Paternostro
Editor: Jennifer Lombardo

Cataloging-in-Publication Data

Names: Washburne, Sophie.
Title: Steve Jobs: computer visionary / Sophie Washburne.
Description: New York : Lucent Press, 2017. | Series: People in the news |
Includes index.
Identifiers: ISBN 9781534560314 (library bound) | ISBN 9781534560321 (ebook)
Subjects: LCSH: Jobs, Steve, 1955-2011–Juvenile literature. | Apple Computer,
Inc.–History–Juvenile literature. | Computer engineers–United States–Biography–
Juvenile literature. | Businessmen–United States–Biography–Juvenile literature.
Classification: LCC QA76.2.A2 W37 2017 | DDC 338.7′6100416092–dc23

Printed in the United States of America

CPSIA compliance information: Batch #CW17KL: For further information contact Greenhaven Publishing LLC, New York,
New York at 1-844-317-7404.

Please visit our website, www.greenhavenpublishing.com. For a free color
catalog of all our high-quality books, call toll free 1-844-317-7404
or fax 1-844-317-7405.

Contents

Foreword

We live in a world where the latest news is always available and where it seems we have unlimited access to the lives of the people in the news. Entire television networks are devoted to news about politics, sports, and entertainment. Social media has allowed people to have an unprecedented level of interaction with celebrities. We have more information at our fingertips than ever before. However, how much do we really know about the people we see on television news programs, social media feeds, and magazine covers?

Despite the constant stream of news, the full stories behind the lives of some of the world's most newsworthy men and women are often unknown. Who was Taylor Swift before she was a pop music phenomenon? What does LeBron James do when he is not playing basketball? What inspired Elon Musk to dream as big as he does?

This series aims to answer questions such as these about some of the biggest names in pop culture, sports, politics, and technology. While the subjects of this series come from all walks of life and areas of expertise, they share a common magnetism that has made them all captivating figures in the public eye. They have shaped the world in some unique way, and—in many cases—they are poised to continue to shape the world for many years to come.

These biographies are not just a collection of basic facts. They tell compelling stories that show how each figure grew to become a powerful public personality. Each book aims to paint a complete, realistic picture of its subject—from the challenges they overcame to the controversies they caused. In doing so, each book reinforces the idea that even the most famous faces on the news are real people who are much more complex than we are often shown in brief video clips or sound bites. Readers are also reminded that there is even more to a person than what they present to the world through social media posts, press releases, and interviews. The whole story of a person's life can only be discovered by digging beneath the surface of their public persona, and that is what this series allows readers to do.

The books in this series are filled with enlightening quotes from speeches and interviews given by the subjects, as well as quotes and anecdotes from those who know their story best: family, friends, coaches, and colleagues. All quotes are noted to provide guidance for further research. Detailed lists of additional resources are also included, as are timelines, indexes, and unique photographs. These text features come together to enhance the reading experience and encourage readers to dive deeper into the stories of these influential men and women.

Fame can be fleeting, but the subjects featured in this series have real staying power. They have fundamentally impacted their respective fields and have achieved great success through hard work and true talent. They are men and women defined by their accomplishments, and they are often seen as role models for the next generation. They have left their mark on the world in a major way, and their stories are meant to inspire readers to leave their mark, too.

Introduction

An Influential Man

Steve Jobs was widely known as the co-founder of Apple and CEO of Pixar. He is often described as the inventor of many things, including personal computers, touchscreen devices, and portable MP3 players. In truth, he did not invent these things, but they would not have been brought into the world without his help. He was someone with big ideas and the determination to go after what he wanted. However, the same qualities that made him a success also made him a controversial figure. Less than a month after his death in 2011, a biography simply titled *Steve Jobs* was published that talked about not just Jobs's achievements, but also the way he was often cruel to his employees and family. *Forbes* magazine stated that people often put up with his behavior because he "was more than a jerk … he was a genius with what seemed like absolute self-confidence and the ability to make his tech dreams—and some of ours—come true."[1] The question people need to ask when talking about Steve Jobs is: Does his success justify the way he achieved it?

Steve Jobs achieved many things, but he was often cruel to the people around him in his pursuit of greatness.

An Early Genius

A man with many sides, Jobs has been described as charming, egotistical, brilliant, opinionated, charismatic, stubborn, persuasive, and critical. He was not easy to understand. Many people found him mysterious. However, one thing is clear: Steve Jobs was not an ordinary person. In 1976, at age 21, he co-founded Apple Computer, Inc. in his parents' garage. Four years later he was worth more than $200 million. By the time he was 30, he had lost his job at Apple. Down but not out, he started another computer company and bought Pixar, the computer graphics division of a movie studio. Pixar made Jobs a billionaire. However, things were not as rosy at Apple. Without Jobs's vision, Apple struggled. On the edge of bankruptcy, the company brought Jobs back in 1997. In a short time, he made Apple more successful than ever.

Jobs's life story is indeed extraordinary. Even as a child, he stood out. He was smarter, wilder, and more of a risk taker than his peers. His interests were also different. His passion was electronics, which set him apart. Throughout most of his youth, he did not fit into the various groups that his classmates formed. Unlike many young people who try to change themselves to fit in, Steve did not mind being different. In fact, he reveled in it. "Think Different," which became Apple's trademark slogan, appropriately described the company's founder, who never shied away from doing just that. Terry Anzur, Steve's high school classmate, recalled: "He ... [made] a statement in the senior talent contest by putting on a laser light show at a time when most of us had never even heard of lasers. He followed his own path, and that made him kind of an outsider with those who followed the crowd."[2]

When Jobs started Apple with his friend Steve Wozniak, many people laughed at them. They said the two men were too young and inexperienced to run a business. The pair had no money, no place to work, and no experience. Although Wozniak was cautious, Jobs had a dream. He believed in himself and the company he was starting. He ignored his critics, persuaded Wozniak to do the same, and followed his heart. According to authors Jeffrey S. Young and William L. Simon, Jobs was "too young and

Steve Wozniak used his skill with electronics to build many of the products Apple sold.

definitely too inexperienced to know what he couldn't achieve, and ruled by the passion of ideas, he had no sense of why something was impossible. This made him willing to try things that wiser people would have said couldn't be done."[3]

Jobs's dream of how that business would change the world was even more outrageous. He believed that computers should be tools for everyday people. Before 1975, computers were huge, complicated, expensive devices that were mainly used by government agencies, universities, and large businesses. Few ordinary people could afford a computer or knew how to use one.

Jobs wanted to change that. He believed that if computers were small enough to sit on a desk, easy to use, attractive, and affordable, people would feel comfortable having the machines in their homes and would use them to do things such as writing letters, keeping address lists, balancing checkbooks, playing games, and drawing pictures. As Apple grew, Jobs's vision of what people could use computers for also grew.

Many industry experts thought Jobs's dream of personal computers was impractical and unmarketable. Jobs proved them wrong. *TIME* magazine reported in 2014, "The Mac is the only personal computer with a 30-year history. Other than Apple itself, the leading computer companies of 1984 included names such as Atari, Commodore, Compaq, Kaypro, and Radio Shack—all of which have since either left the PC business or vanished altogether ... That the Mac has not only survived but thrived is astonishing."[4]

More to Accomplish

Despite Apple's tremendous success, much of which was due to Jobs, after 10 years, a power struggle ensued, and he was fired from the company he had started. Having already achieved more than most people ever dream of, Jobs could have rested on his accomplishments. In fact, his friends advised him to retire. However, he remained true to himself. He loved his work and believed he had more to contribute, so he invested in two more companies—NeXT computers and Pixar. Most experts predicted he would fail. Once again, Jobs proved them wrong. Addressing the 2005 graduating class of Stanford University, Jobs explained: "I'm convinced that the only thing that kept me going was that I loved what I did. You've got to find what you love … Your work is going to fill a large part of your life and the only way to be truly satisfied is to do what you believe is great work. And the only way to do great work is to love what you do … Don't settle."[5]

Steve Jobs never settled. He refused to change in order fit in. He remained dedicated to his ideas despite the doubt of others, and he went forward after being fired from Apple rather than settling for the easy life.

However, there is a dark side to his success: the way he treated his employees and other companies that he worked with. He was willing to be cruel to people, refuse to pay them what they deserved, and break contracts with companies who were relying on the income he had promised them. In his private life, too, his decisions could sometimes be called dishonorable. For example, when he was 23, he and his girlfriend had a baby, but he refused for years to admit that his daughter was his. However, he did later say that he regretted the way he had handled the situation.

Jobs always remained true to himself—even when that self was not pleasant. "Your time is limited," he told the Stanford graduates, "so don't waste it living someone else's life. Don't be trapped by dogma—which is living with the results of other people's thinking. Don't let the noise of other's opinions drown out your own inner voice. And most important, have the courage to follow your heart."[6] This is exactly what Steve Jobs did. In the process, he changed the world.

Chapter **One**

Pranks and Electronics

Steve Jobs was born on February 24, 1955. His parents were not married, and they placed him for adoption. Clara and Paul Jobs adopted him, and his birth mother made them promise to send him to college one day. Although he eventually dropped out, those classes and the people he met there had an impact on the company he would one day start.

The Jobs family—which eventually included Patty, an adopted daughter—lived in California. When Steve was five years old, they moved to a town called Mountain View. It is located in what came to be known as Silicon Valley, where many of the world's most important tech companies were started. Being around so many other people who were interested in technology and creating new things undoubtedly influenced Steve. He was a great marketer and visionary—a person who could imagine things that didn't exist yet—but he did not have the skills to build the things he thought of. Living in a town with so many people who did have those skills certainly helped Apple get its start.

Stubborn from Youth

From the beginning, Steve was a handful. Even at a young age, he demonstrated the intensity, strength of will, and desire to set the rules that he would later become known for. For example, as a toddler, he woke up at 4 a.m. every morning, ready to play. Although his parents repeatedly ordered him to go back to bed, he refused. Realizing it was pointless to fight the headstrong child, his parents bought him a rocking horse and record player stocked with rock and roll records. This kept him entertained while the rest of the family slept.

On other occasions, his willfulness got him into trouble. For instance, although he was frequently warned against it, he could not restrain himself from sticking a bobby pin into an electrical outlet. The trip to the emergency room that followed did not stop him from later swallowing ant poison, even though he was not supposed to go near it. However, when he wanted to be, he could be very charming and persuasive, and he convinced his friends to pull many pranks with him. His coworkers at Apple said that Steve could convince anyone to do practically anything, no matter how dangerous or outrageous. "The joke going around said that Jobs had a reality distortion field surrounding him," author Robert X. Cringely explained. "He'd say something and the kids in the Macintosh division would find themselves replying, 'Drink poison Kool-Aid? Yeah, that makes sense.'"[7]

The Importance of Mentors

To keep Steve out of trouble, his father made an effort to spend time with him. Paul Jobs was a mechanical whiz. In his spare time, he bought wrecked cars from junkyards. He rebuilt the cars in his garage workshop and resold them at a profit. Steve spent many hours at his dad's side learning about mechanics, electronics, and business. He recalled:

> I was very lucky. My father, Paul, was a pretty remarkable man
> … He was a machinist by trade and worked very hard and was
> kind of a genius with his hands. He had a workbench out in the
> garage where, when I was about five or six, he sectioned off a
> little piece of it and said "Steve, this is your workbench now." And
> he gave me some of his smaller tools and showed me how to
> use a hammer and saw and how to build things. It was really
> good for me. He spent a lot of time with me teaching me how
> to build things, how to take things apart, put things back
> together. One of the things he touched upon was electronics.
> He did not have a deep understanding of electronics himself
> but he'd encountered electronics a lot in automobiles and other
> things he would fix. He showed me the [basics] of electronics
> and I got very interested in that.[8]

Many of their neighbors were engineers who had garage workshops where they tinkered with electronic projects. One man in particular, Larry Lange, who was an electrical engineer, took Steve under his wing. Lange had a carbon microphone, which produced sound without an amplifier. The device fascinated Steve. He spent hours questioning Lange about how the device worked. Steve was so single-minded in his interest that Lange eventually gave Steve the microphone so he could take it apart and study it.

Lange also got Steve interested in building Heathkits. These were kits that provided electronic hobbyists with easy-to-follow instructions and parts so that they could build their own radios, hi-fi equipment, oscilloscopes, and other electronic devices. Jobs recalled:

> Heathkits were really great … These Heathkits would come with
> these detailed manuals about how to put this thing together and
> all the parts would be laid out in a certain way and color coded.
> You'd actually build this thing yourself. I would say that this gave

Steve Jobs used Heathkits to build electronics similar to this amplifier.

one several things. It gave one an understanding of what was inside a finished product and how it worked because it would include a theory of operation, but maybe more importantly, it gave one the sense that one could build the things that one saw around oneself in the universe. These things were not mysteries anymore. I mean you looked at a television set [and] you would think that "I haven't built one of those, but I could ..." It gave a tremendous level of self-confidence, that through exploration and learning one could understand seemingly complex things in one's environment. My childhood was very fortunate in that way.[9]

Getting on the Right Track

Steve's fourth grade teacher, Imogene "Teddy" Hill, had a lasting influence on his life. She realized that Steve had a lot of energy that needed to be channeled into learning. However, he was rebellious and often refused to do his assignments. To gain his interest, Hill bribed him with candy and money. Once she sparked his interest, she gave him special assignments such as building a camera. In an interview with the Smithsonian Institution, Jobs talked about the impact Hill had on him:

> I had such respect for her that it sort of re-ignited my desire to learn ... I think I probably learned more academically in that one year than I learned in my life. I'm 100% sure that if it hadn't been for Mrs. Hill ... I would have absolutely ended up in jail. I could see those tendencies in myself to have a certain energy to do something. It could have been directed at doing something interesting that other people thought was a good idea or doing something interesting that maybe other people didn't like so much. When you're young, a little bit of course correction goes a long way.[1]

1. Quoted in Smithsonian Institution Oral and Video Histories, "Steve Jobs," April 20, 1995. http://americanhistory.si.edu/collections/comphist/sj1.html.

Too Smart for School

Spending time with his dad and Larry Lange kept Steve occupied at home, but school bored him. Intellectually, Steve was far ahead of his classmates and did not relate well to them. His mother had taught him to read when he was still a toddler. Indeed, he was already working on electronics projects while his peers were still learning their ABCs. Jeff Eastwood, one of Steve's neighbors and schoolmates, explained: "We couldn't understand what he was talking about half the time. He'd show me things that I couldn't understand with all the electronic gear that he'd taken apart."[10]

Steve's high intelligence combined with his desire to set his own rules led to trouble. He did not obey his teachers if he did not agree with them. For instance, he often refused to do schoolwork that he had already mastered, saying that he did not see the point. When he did do his work, he usually finished long before the other students. To entertain himself, he invented complex practical jokes, which he pulled on his classmates and teachers. Such pranks, according to Kaplan, "were a way to show intellectual prowess and rebellion at the same time."[11]

He let snakes loose in the classroom and set off explosives under the teacher's chair. One of his more complicated tricks involved bicycles. He managed to persuade his classmates to give him the combinations of their bicycle locks. Then, with the help of another intellectually gifted boy, Steve switched the locks on all the bicycles, making it impossible for the other children to unlock their bicycles. "There was this big bike rack where everybody put their bikes, maybe a hundred bikes in this rack, and we traded everybody our lock combination for theirs on an individual basis and then went out one day and put everybody's lock on everybody else's bike and it took them until ten o'clock that night to get all the bikes sorted out,"[12] Steve recalled.

As a result of all his mischief, Steve was often suspended from school. His teachers thought the best way to keep him out of trouble was to challenge him academically. To determine the best way to do this, Steve was given an intelligence test at the end of the fourth grade. It showed that, intellectually, he was functioning on a high school level. The school recommended that Steve skip fifth and sixth grades and go straight to seventh.

Steve's parents resisted. Although their son was intellectually advanced, they knew that, socially and physically, he was still a child. They did, however, agree to allow him to skip the fifth grade. This meant he would start middle school a year early.

His new school was a rough place with many tough, streetwise students. The police were often called to break up fights. Little learning went on there, and Steve hated the place. To make matters worse, Steve became the target of bullies. He was so miserable at the school that upon finishing sixth grade, he threatened to drop out of school if he had to go back there. He was so determined that his parents moved the family to Los Altos, another town in Silicon Valley, just so Steve could go to a different school. "At eleven years old," authors Jeffrey S. Young and William L. Simon observed, "Steve was already able to demonstrate enough strength of will to convince his parents to resettle. His trademark intensity, the single-mindedness that he could apply to remove any obstacle in his path, was already evident."[13]

The move was good for Steve in many ways. His new school offered advanced classes, so he was intellectually challenged. Although he did not fit in with any group, he was not harassed there. His parents tried to help him make friends by enrolling him on a swim team. Steve was not naturally athletic, but he was a good swimmer. Despite his skill, he did not fit in there either. He did not like being part of a team, and he was so intense about winning that he made the other boys uncomfortable. "He was pretty much a crybaby. He'd lose a race and go off and cry. He didn't quite fit in with everyone else. He wasn't one of the guys,"[14] Mark Wozniak, Jobs's former teammate and the brother of his future partner Steve Wozniak, explained.

Fortunately, Steve did not mind being an outsider. He liked being seen as different, and he thought of himself as a rebel. Also, he was not completely alone at school. He made friends with another outsider, Bill Fernandez, who shared his passion for electronics. Outside of school, Los Altos contained even more engineers and electronic hobbyists than Mountain View. Bill already knew many of these people and took Steve into their garage workshops. They were happy to share their knowledge and spare electronic parts with the boys. Fernandez explained:

If you grow up in a woodworking community, with all the tools and professional woodworking around you, and everyone on the block is talking about woodcarving all the time, don't you think the kids will turn out to be good woodworkers? We grew up in a town, on streets ... and [working in] garages where all

Steve often worked in garage workshops when he was not in school.

Steve's First Job

When Steve was in high school, he joined a club called the Hewlett-Packard (HP) Explorers Club, where engineers from HP would give lessons on things they were doing at work. Steve loved it, and the club inspired him to work on his own computer projects. In the biography *Steve Jobs*, Walter Isaacson describes how Steve's go-getter attitude got him big rewards, even as a teenager:

> *Jobs decided to build a frequency counter, which measures the number of pulses per second in an electronic signal. He needed some parts that HP made, so he picked up the phone and called the CEO. "Back then, people didn't have unlisted numbers. So I looked up Bill Hewlitt in Palo Alto and called him at home. And he answered and chatted with me for twenty minutes. He got me the parts, but he also got me a job in the plant where they made frequency counters." Jobs worked there the summer after his freshman year at Homestead High.*[1]

1. Walter Isaacson, *Steve Jobs*, New York, NY: Simon & Schuster, 2011, e-book.

we had were the tools for electronics. Isn't it natural that we ended up being pretty good at it, being involved with electronics, doing something in that field?[15]

A Great Friendship

In 1968, when Steve was a freshman at Homestead High School, Fernandez introduced him to his neighbor, an older

Steve Wozniak and Steve Jobs started Apple together when they were in their 20s.

boy named Steve Wozniak. Woz, as he was known, was a college freshman. He loved electronics and pulling pranks. When Woz and Jobs met, Woz was trying to build a computer-like device from a plan he designed on paper. The device was a very basic, early calculator that could multiply numbers and give the results in binary code, which uses only the numerals 1 and 0.

Fernandez helped Woz build the device and wanted to show the machine to Jobs, as well as introduce him to Woz. From the start, the two Steves hit it off. Woz recalled:

I remember—Bill called Steve and had him come over to his house. I remember Steve and I just sat on the sidewalk in front of Bill's house for the longest time just sharing stories—mostly about pranks we'd pulled, and also what kind of electronic designs we'd done … So Steve came into the garage and saw the computer … and listened to our description of it. I could tell he was impressed. I mean, we'd actually built a computer from scratch and proved that it was possible—or going to be possible—for people to have computers in a really small space. Steve and I got close right away, even though he was still in high school.[16]

It did not take long for the two Steves to become close friends. Working on projects with Woz and Fernandez increased Steve's passion for electronics, and the three enjoyed using their knowledge of electronics to play pranks together. Steve joined the electronics club at Homestead High School, as well as Hewlett-Packard's Explorers Club, which offered monthly lectures for young people interested in electronics.

The Beginning of a Partnership

Steve and Woz's first real project together was building an illegal device known as a blue box. It allowed users to make free long-distance telephone calls. The pair built one for the challenge of it, and it worked. Steve, already showing that he was an entrepreneur, realized that they would be able to build a lot of blue boxes and sell them to college students at the University of California at Berkeley, where Woz was taking classes. They demonstrated how the boxes worked by calling The Ritz London hotel and making reservations for dozens of nonexistent people. Once, just for fun, they called the pope at the Vatican.

Both Steves contributed to the project in their own way. Jobs got the supplies for the boxes for $40. Woz built the devices. Jobs sold them for anywhere from $150 to $300, depending

The first item Wozniak and Jobs sold together was an illegal blue box that could make free long-distance calls.

on how much he thought the customer could afford. Together, they made and sold about 100 blue boxes.

Their illegal enterprise came to an end after Jobs was held up at gunpoint by a prospective buyer. However, the pattern that the two young men established of Woz building a product and Jobs marketing it would serve them well in the future. As Jobs pointed out in his biography, "If it hadn't been for the blue boxes, there wouldn't have been an Apple … I'm 100 percent sure of that. Woz and I learned how to work together, and we gained the confidence that we could solve technical problems and actually put something into production."[17]

Chapter Two

Spiritual and Technological Experiments

Around the end of his high school career, Steve Jobs started experimenting with drugs and fad diets. He smoked marijuana, took acid, and ate only fruits and vegetables. He and his father had many fights about this lifestyle, but Jobs refused to listen; he would walk out of the arguments and continue doing whatever he wanted, even though he knew it upset his parents.

As a senior, Jobs met and started dating Chrisann Brennan, a girl in the junior class of his school. They moved in together after graduation, against his parents' wishes. Their relationship was complicated, and they dated on and off for many years. According to Walter Isaacson, Jobs's biographer, "He could be brutally cold and rude to her at times, but he was also entrancing and able to impose his will. 'He was an enlightened being who was cruel,' [Chrisann] recalled. 'That's a strange combination.'"[18] He would do things such as send her love letters one day and tell her that she had too many wrinkles the next.

Right after graduation, Jobs was not sure he wanted to go to college, but his parents had promised his birth mother that they would send him. When his parents pushed him, he applied to Reed College, one of the most expensive in the country, which was known for its oddball students and liberal counterculture atmosphere. He told his parents, who had agreed to pay for college, that he would not go anywhere except Reed. Although they were unhappy about it, they wanted him to go to college, so they agreed. In the end, they emptied out their savings so Jobs could have his way. When they dropped him off, he walked away without saying goodbye or thank you—something that he regretted as an adult.

Life at College

Even at Reed, where many of the students were brilliant and strange, Jobs stood out. Robert Friedland, who became Jobs's friend, recalled:

> He was always walking around barefoot. He was one of the freaks on the campus. The thing that struck me was his intensity. Whatever he was interested in he would generally carry to an irrational extreme. He wasn't a rapper [talker]. One of his numbers was to stare at the person he was talking to. He would stare into their ... eyeballs, ask some question and would want a response without the other person averting their eyes.[19]

Friedland had a huge impact on Jobs; he was older than Jobs and was somewhat of a celebrity on campus, partially because he had previously been arrested for possession of a large amount of the drug LSD. Jobs first noticed Friedland because he typically dressed in long, flowing robes.

Friedland was an outgoing person who could charm almost anyone. He was always the center of attention and was an excellent salesman. He was especially good at captivating a crowd and was elected the president of Reed's student council. He soon became Jobs's mentor.

Jobs was an introvert who had trouble connecting with large groups. Because he often felt that he was smarter than almost everyone else, he sometimes came off as arrogant, which did not make other people like him. Jobs studied the way Friedland interacted with people and how he captivated large crowds. By imitating Friedland, Jobs became more charming and better able to address a large group. This skill served him well when he addressed MacWorld gatherings in the future. According to Daniel Kottke, who became one of Jobs's closest friends at Reed,

> Robert was very much an outgoing, charismatic guy, a real sales-man … When I first met Steve he was shy … I think Robert taught him a lot about selling, about coming out of his shell, of opening up and taking charge of a situation. Robert was one of those guys who was always the center of attention. He'd walk into a room and you would instantly notice him. Steve was the absolute opposite when he came to Reed. After he spent time with Robert, some of it started to rub off.[20]

Trying Different Lifestyles

Friedland also inspired Jobs to try different lifestyles so he could figure out which one he liked best. Jobs conducted his search for enlightenment with the same intensity as he had conducted his electronic projects. He studied Eastern religions and became a Zen Buddhist, a religion he continued to practice for the rest of his life. This religion focuses on simplicity, which later influenced how simple and user-friendly Apple products are. He tried meditating, experimented with sleep deprivation, and studied the link between diet and physical and spiritual health. He experimented with fasting and different kinds of extreme diets, and he campaigned for his friends to join him on whatever diet he was currently following. At one point, his diet consisted mainly of carrots. He ate so many that his skin turned orange. He again became a fruitarian—someone who eats only fruit and vegetables—and took to showering infrequently because he believed his diet would keep his body clean. For a while, he had problems keeping food down because he was starving himself, so when

The apples Jobs harvested on the All One Farm were the inspiration for the computer company's name.

he did eat, his body wasn't used to it. "I still believe man is a fruitarian," he told writer Michael Moritz years later. "Of course, back then I got into it in my typically nutso way."[21] Eventually, he became a vegetarian and followed that diet for the rest of his life.

Jobs also spent a lot of time on Friedland's farm, called the All One Farm, which was run as a commune—a community that all the members help run by doing work. At first, Jobs liked the non-materialistic lifestyle, where people were paid for their work with food and a place to stay. However, he soon realized that Friedland was making money off of the community members' work by selling the apples they harvested and the wood they chopped. Jobs went to the farm less often and trusted Friedland less after that.

An Unusual Approach

After one semester at Reed, Jobs dropped out; he didn't like most of the classes he was taking, and he felt guilty for wasting his parents' money on something he didn't feel was helping him. Unlike most college dropouts, he did not leave the campus or stop attending all his classes. He just stopped paying tuition and dorm fees. With his characteristic rebelliousness, he decided he could have the same experience for free. He slept on the floor of Kottke's dorm room and attended classes in subjects that interested him without getting credit for them. He made friends with the dean of students, Jack Dudman, who was so impressed with the young man that he tolerated Jobs's actions. Dudman explained: "Steve had a very inquiring mind that was enormously attractive. You wouldn't get away with bland statements. He refused to accept automatically perceived truths. He wanted to examine everything himself."[22]

In this manner, Jobs was able to satisfy his intellectual curiosity without being forced to sit through required classes that did not interest him. Instead, he attended classes that he might not have experienced had he followed a standard course of study. For instance, he attended a calligraphy class, which influenced his idea that Apple computers would have multiple fonts.

The calligraphy class Jobs took was a big part of the reason why computers have different fonts today.

The Beginning of the Technology Era

Many of the changes that began in the 1960s—a decade marked by social upheaval—continued to grow in the 1970s. For instance, the hippie culture, which rejected traditional social values and materialism, continued into the early part of the 1970s. Hippies were trying to change society while experimenting with alternative lifestyles, such as communal living, vegetarianism, Eastern religions such as Zen Buddhism, and using psychedelic drugs. The environmental movement also became popular in the 1970s.

The 1970s also witnessed an explosion in technology. The laser, integrated circuit, microprocessor, personal computer, floppy disk, ink-jet printer, pocket calculator, video game, microwave oven, and video cassette recorder all were developed in the 1970s. The fiber optics industry, which transformed communications forever, also began in the 1970s.

Zen Buddhism is a religion that values simplicity, which inspired the way Jobs designed Apple products.

Jobs recalled:

After six months … I had no idea what I wanted to do with my life and no idea how college was going to help me figure it out. And here I was spending all of the money my parents had saved their entire life. So I decided to drop out and trust that it would all work out OK. It was pretty scary at the time, but looking back it was one of the best decisions I ever made. The minute I dropped out I could stop taking the required classes that didn't interest me, and begin dropping in on the ones that looked interesting. It wasn't all romantic. I didn't have a dorm room, so I slept on the floor in friends' rooms, I returned Coke bottles for the 5-cent deposits to buy food with, and I would walk the 7 miles across town every Sunday night to get one good meal a week at the Hare Krishna temple. I loved it. And much of what I stumbled into by following my curiosity and intuition turned out to be priceless later on.[23]

Motivation Pays Off

In 1973, Robert Friedland went to India. There, he claimed, he had finally found the meaning of life. Jobs wanted to go to India, too, and he wanted Dan Kottke to join him. To earn enough money to make the trip, Jobs left Reed and moved back home with his parents. He got a job working for Atari, which, at the time, was a small company that made video games for arcades. Jobs's job was to examine newly designed games and make improvements to them, such as adding sound and correcting glitches. It was the type of work normally done by an engineer. According to Wozniak, the job was "like modifying a program to do different things, just barely a step under designing them yourself and a step that all design engineers go through."[24]

Jobs was not highly qualified for the job, but he managed to

Jobs worked for Atari, an early video game company, to pay for his trip to India. Shown here is an early Atari computer game system.

talk his way into it by walking into the building and threatening not to leave until he was hired. Al Alcorn, Atari's co-founder, recalled that Jobs was

> *dressed in rags, basically, hippie stuff. An eighteen-year-old drop-out of Reed College. I don't know why I hired him, except that he was determined to have the job and there was some spark. I really saw the spark in that man, some inner energy, an attitude that he was going to get it done. And he had a vision, too. You know the definition of a visionary is "someone with an inner vision not supported by external facts," he had those great ideas without much to back them up. Except that he believed in them.*[25]

The other engineers in the company did not like working with Jobs. They complained that he was strange and smelled, which was because he still thought his diet meant he did not have to shower often. However, Alcorn insisted on keeping him and arranged it so that Steve worked at night when no one else was present. One exception was Ron Wayne, a coworker who had previously tried to start his own company. The business failed, but he was the first person Jobs had ever met who had tried to start a business, and that showed him it was possible for anyone to start their own business.

In Search of Enlightenment

After he had worked at Atari for a few months, Jobs told his boss that he was quitting to go to India, and he asked Alcorn to pay for the flight. Alcorn told him that he would not pay for all of it, but he offered to send Jobs to Europe so the flight to India would be cheaper. The company needed someone to go to Germany to repair some of their video games there. Jobs spent a few weeks in Europe, and then he proceeded on to India, where Kottke joined him several weeks later.

Jobs and Kottke spent about seven months together in India. Their goal was to go to the village of Kainchi to meet Neem Karoli Baba, Friedland's guru, whom Jobs hoped would help him achieve spiritual enlightenment. When they got to Kainchi, they found out that the guru was dead, so they tried to find enlightenment on their own by wandering and living simply. They had their heads shaved, traveled the country on foot, begged for food, slept in abandoned buildings or out in the open, and attended religious festivals.

Jobs considered seeking out another guru, but he did not do so. He had not found the answers he was looking for in India. He returned to the United States, still searching for answers. He spent time at the All One Farm and tried different kinds of therapy. Eventually, he met a spiritual leader named Kobun Chino Otogawa and became very devoted to him and his teachings.

Jobs and Kottke searched for enlightenment in India.

Computer Terms

The world of computers has a language all its own. Here are a few computer terms and their meanings:

application or app: A software program that runs on a computer.

BASIC: A popular computer programming language used in the creation of software.

bit: The smallest unit of data in a computer.

byte: A unit of data equal to eight bits. Bytes are used to measure file size and computer memory.

Central Processing Unit (CPU): The chip that instructs the computer how to run. It is basically the brain of the computer.

chip or microchip: A tiny electronic device whose circuitry acts as memory for the computer.

data: Information stored or processed on a computer.

hardware: The actual computer and the parts that comprise it.

motherboard: The circuit board within a computer.

Random Access Memory (RAM): The memory available to computer programs. For instance, a computer with 10 MB RAM has 10 million bytes of memory.

software: A general term for programs that can be run on a computer.

Getting Ahead by Cheating

When he returned from India, Jobs went back to work at Atari and reconnected with Woz, whom he hadn't seen much since he started college. Jobs often brought his friend into work with him. Woz loved checking out the new games and helped Jobs with his work just for the fun of it. "The best thing about hiring Jobs," Alcorn admitted, "is that he brought along Woz to visit a lot."[26]

Atari was the creator of Pong, an early two-player video game based on ping-pong. The company wanted to develop a similar one-player game called Breakout, and they wanted to use the fewest computer chips possible. They told Jobs they would pay him $700 to build the prototype, with a bonus if he used fewer than 50 chips.

In reality, Jobs did not have the technical skill to create such a game from scratch, but Woz did. Jobs promised to pay his friend half if he would design the game. Working as a team, the two produced Breakout in only four nights, using only 45 chips. The game was exactly what Atari wanted. Wozniak designed it based on the description the game designers gave him, while Jobs put all the wires and components of the game together.

Jobs told Woz that Atari paid him $700 for the game. He then paid Woz half, or $350. He kept the bonus for himself without telling Woz about it. It is unclear why he did this; in his official biography, Jobs denied ever having done such a thing, but several people at Atari confirmed that they did pay him a bonus that Woz never received. "I think Steve needed the money, and he just didn't tell me the truth," Wozniak said. He continued:

> I wish he had just been honest. If he had told me he needed the money, he should have known I would have just given it to him. He was a friend. You help friends … Ethics always mattered to me, and I still don't understand why he would've gotten paid one thing and told me he'd gotten paid another … But, you know, people are different.[27]

This incident shows that Jobs had no problem being untruthful

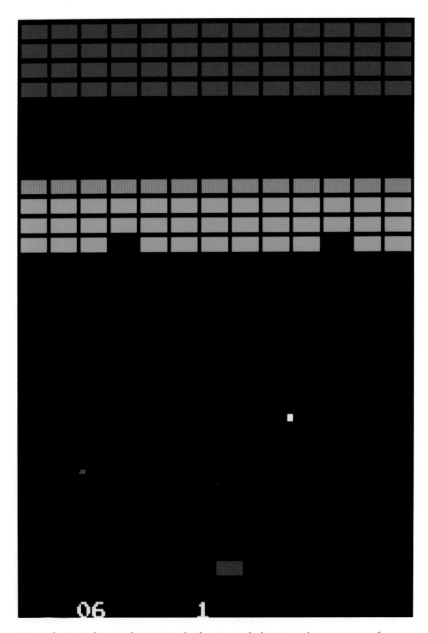

Together, Jobs and Wozniak designed the Breakout game for Atari. A screenshot of the game is shown here.

when it suited his needs. It was partially this ruthlessness and dishonesty that helped him get ahead in the business world, but he could also be generous when he wanted to be. For instance, in India, when Kottke's money was stolen, Jobs paid for his food and travel expenses so Kottke could get back to the airport safely.

A Turning Point

In the spring of 1975, Woz joined a group called the Homebrew Computer Club. It was an electronics club whose members were engineers and electronic hobbyists interested in computers. The club gave them a chance to share their ideas and electronic creations. According to Moritz, "The Homebrew Club provided an audience for … [individuals] like Wozniak, whose primary interest in life was something that most people couldn't understand … In later years the club was fondly remembered as a movable science fair where like-minded souls gathered to share their secrets, display their machines, and distribute schematics."[28] Many of the members were trying to build their own computers, including Woz, who had an idea for a new kind of computer.

Back then, computers were gigantic devices. Personal computers—or microcomputers, as they were known at the time—came unassembled in kit form. They had no monitor or keyboard. Instead, they had switches and lights that the user flipped to program. "Every computer up to that time looked like an airplane cockpit … with switches and lights you had to manipulate and read,"[29] Wozniak explained. He envisioned a completely different kind of computer that worked with a television and a typewriter-like keyboard. Users would type in commands, which would appear on the television screen, or monitor.

Jobs was fascinated by Woz's vision. Although he was not capable of building such a device himself, he was confident that if anyone could build it, it was Wozniak. Jobs did everything he could to help his friend succeed, including coming up with ideas such as adding a disk for storage, which would be included in Apple computers in the future. He also convinced engineers at

Personal computers looked very different in the 1970s than they do today.

Intel, an electronics company, to donate rare and expensive computer chips for the project, without which it is unlikely that Woz would have succeeded. "He made some calls and by some marketing miracle he was able to score some free DRAMs [dynamic random access memory chips] from Intel—unbelievable considering their price and rarity at the time. Steve is just that sort of person," Wozniak explained. "I mean, he knew how to talk to a sales representative. I could never have done that; I was too shy. But he got me Intel DRAM chips."[30]

For the first time in a long time, Jobs did not feel lost. He believed that helping Woz build a computer was more important to the world than his own previous efforts to gain enlightenment. Steve Jobs had found where he belonged and what he was meant to do.

Chapter Three

The Start of
an Empire

Woz worked on his computer for months, getting cheap parts where he could and writing the code by hand. It did not look much like modern computers; it was a circuit board connected to a television set and a keyboard. Finally, he was ready to test it. On June 29, 1975, he typed letters on the keyboard and they appeared on the screen in front of him. This was the first time in history this had ever happened. On the old computers, which were big enough to take up an entire room, information was put into the computer on punched paper cards, and the results were printed out up to a day later. There were no screens at all, and only experts in computer programming could operate them.

Jobs started going to Homebrew Computer Club meetings with Woz, and he saw how interested people were in Woz's computer. The club members liked to share their work, and Woz would happily have given his ideas away for free so they could help other people with their own inventions. Jobs was the one who came up with the idea of selling things. He suggested that Woz stop showing people his notes and instead create and sell printed circuit boards (PCBs) made to Woz's design. Electrical engineer Ryan Schaub explained: "PCBs were already being used, but Wozniak's designs were smaller and cheaper than people could

The first computers were large and complicated. Jobs and Wozniak wanted to make them smaller and simpler.

find elsewhere."[31] Wozniak told Isaacson, "Every time I'd design something great, Steve would find a way to make money for us."[32] Jobs did not have Woz's technical ability, and Woz did not have Jobs's ambition or business sense. Their combined skills and partnership made Apple possible.

A Great Adventure

When Jobs first suggested he and Wozniak build and sell the circuit boards, Woz was reluctant. He had no thoughts of starting a business, getting rich, or changing the world. Nor did he see how such a business could make money. Although he was not materialistic, he did not have money to lose. Jobs, with his typical intensity, was sure there was a need for such a business. Electronic hobbyists, he insisted, would buy the device. Also, if the business failed, at least they could say they had tried.

Wozniak recalled:

> His idea was for us to make these preprinted circuit boards for $20 and sell them for $40 ... Frankly, I couldn't see how we would earn our money back ... But Steve had a good argument. ... He said—and I can remember him saying this like it was yesterday: "Well, even if we lose our money, we'll have a company. For once in our lives, we'll have a company." ... That convinced me. And I was excited to think about us like that. To be two best friends starting a company. Wow. I knew right then that I'd do it. How could I not?[33]

Once the two agreed on selling the circuit boards, they had to come up with a name for the company. Jobs, who had recently visited the All One Farm, suggested Apple Computer. He wanted a name that did not sound too technical and would attract everyday people. Wozniak liked the name. On April 1, 1976, Apple Computer was born.

The First Apple Computer

Starting a new company was not easy, especially for two young men whose only business experience was selling illegal blue boxes. They had to come up with enough money to produce the computers, which they named Apple I. Jobs sold his van for $1,000, while Wozniak sold his calculator for $250. Originally, Woz wanted to keep his job at Hewlett-Packard (HP) and work on Apple in his spare time, but Jobs knew that if Apple was going to become a real company, they both needed to be in it all the

The First PC

The earliest personal computer, or PC, was the Altair 8800. Ed Roberts created the company that made them in his garage in Albuquerque, New Mexico, in 1975. The Altair 8800 arrived as a kit that buyers had to assemble. It had no keyboard, monitor, printer, or mouse, and it only had 256 bytes of memory. That is about the amount of memory a modern computer uses to store one sentence.

The Altair 8800 had switches and lights on the front panel. The user flipped the switches to program the computer, and the lights showed what the computer was doing. For example, to do a math problem, the user would flip specific switches to put in the numbers, and the computer would answer by flashing certain lights.

Although Altair 8800 could not do much, hobbyists liked the challenge of entering commands and seeing if their program actually worked. When they were teenagers, Bill Gates and Paul Allen altered a programming language called BASIC, which had replaced punched cards on early computers. Gates and Allen made BASIC work on the Altair 8800; it allowed users to load the program on paper tape right into the computer rather than flipping switches. This made computers easier to operate and made it possible for them to do more. It was the experiment that started Microsoft.

way. He got his coworker, Ron Wayne, to convince Woz by telling him that "a great engineer would be remembered only if he teamed with a great marketer, and this required him to commit his designs to the partnership."[34] Woz was originally planning to

Jobs and Wozniak called their first computer the Apple I. They assembled and sold the circuit board, and the buyer plugged it into a TV and keyboard.

let HP use his designs, but after Wayne talked to him, he agreed to let only Apple use them. However, he continued to work at HP while Apple was getting started because he was not convinced the company would succeed.

The two planned to make 50 printed circuit boards in all. Then, Jobs got a $25,000 order for 50 fully assembled circuit boards from a local electronics store. The store's owner, Paul Terrell, had seen Wozniak demonstrating his invention at a Homebrew Club meeting. He liked what he saw and told Jobs to stay in touch.

Jobs's idea of staying in touch was going to Terrell's store the very next morning. Terrell was not enthusiastic about stocking just the PCBs, but he thought he could sell fully assembled boards. The difference was that a person who bought a PCB would also have to buy the chips separately to make it work. A fully assembled board—the heart of a computer—would work as soon as someone plugged it in at home. However, a buyer would still have to find his or her own keyboard and monitor. Even though this was not their original plan, Jobs took the order. "That was the biggest single episode in the company's history," explained Wozniak. "Nothing in subsequent years was so great and so unexpected. It was not what we had intended to do."[35]

Producing 50 fully assembled boards meant that Jobs and Wozniak not only had to supply the finished boards, but also buy all the components and parts and put the machines together. With so many computers to make, it was not practical to build the boards by hand. The two decided to have them mass-produced by a manufacturing company. Then, Jobs and Wozniak would plug in the computer chips and do the wiring themselves. However, Woz's drawing of the circuit board was hard for the manufacturer to follow. Jobs asked Wayne to draw the schematics based on Wozniak's plans, to design an owner's manual, and to be the tiebreaker in any disagreements between Jobs and Woz. Because they had no money to pay Wayne, they offered him 10 percent of the company. Wayne agreed, but he did not stay with the company long. He sold back his shares—which became worth $65 million four years later—for $300.

Wayne doubted that Jobs and Wozniak could come up with enough money to pay for all the supplies they needed, and he believed the company would fail. Jobs proved Wayne wrong. He convinced a local electronics supply company to give him parts for 30 days on credit. At the same time, he worked out a deal with Terrell to be paid cash upon delivery of the computers. Each machine cost $220 to make. Terrell paid $500 for each one. When Terrell paid Jobs, Jobs used half the cash to pay off the electronics company. Jobs then invested their profits back into the business.

Humble Beginnings

Jobs kept the location of the company's headquarters under wraps. Unable to afford to rent a space, the boys used the Jobses' garage. To make the business seem more professional, Jobs got a post office box and an answering service, which forwarded calls to his mother. These measures kept potential customers from knowing just how small the business actually was.

The garage was a hub of activity. Jobs and Wozniak, who was still working at HP, stayed up nights working on the computers. Jobs spent his days picking up the finished boards from the manufacturer and acquiring supplies.

They hired their friends Daniel Kottke and Elizabeth Holmes to help them. Soon, Jobs's parents and sister were added to the company's payroll. The group worked round the clock. Holmes kept the accounts, and the others assembled the circuit boards. Wozniak tested each completed board by plugging it into a television set and a keyboard. If there was a problem, he corrected it. From the start, Jobs insisted they use only the best components. While other hobby computers were using static RAM chips (random access memory, or the memory available on a computer) that used a lot of power, he was adamant that Apple use the new Intel DRAM chips. They used up much less power than the old-fashioned chips. Other hobbyists criticized Apple for using the chips, which were more expensive than the static chips. However, Jobs was right about their value. Apple I was the first personal computer to use the chips, which eventually became the industry standard. "Steve was pushing to use the right parts," Wozniak explained. "We were lucky to be on the right track. It was one of the luckiest technology steps on the whole development."[36]

In addition to his other duties, Jobs went to dozens of electronics stores trying to sell Apple I. With his typical determination, he often would not leave until the manager agreed to stock at least one machine. In this manner, he managed to sell 150 additional computers, which he and Woz priced at $666.66. They had no idea of the number's Satanic connection (The

By using more expensive, cutting-edge computer chips, Jobs and Wozniak made Apple products the best on the market.

devil is sometimes represented by the number 666.), picking it because they liked the repeating digits.

Planning for the Future

Apple I was very different from modern computers. It was more a computer kit than a complete computer. It had no keyboard, case, or television monitor. Buyers had to supply these features. It stored data on a cassette tape, and it produced only black and white text and graphics.

Jobs and Wozniak showed Apple I at the Personal Computing Festival in Atlantic City, New Jersey, in August 1976. It was the machine's first national exposure. Their display, which was perched on a wobbly old card table in a dark corner, was not given much attention. The other computers at the convention looked more professional and came with more parts, such as a keyboard and a power supply. The experience made a big impression on Jobs. He realized that if they were going to sell their computers to everyone, not just hobbyists, presentation, design, and marketing were important.

Even before Wozniak had finished designing Apple I, he started thinking of ways to improve it, and while Jobs went to the convention to sell Apple I, Woz spent most of the time in the hotel room working on the next prototype. He wanted his next computer, which he and Jobs named Apple II, to support color, sound, and high-resolution graphics. He also wanted the machine to have slots in the back, which would allow the memory to be expanded. Jobs had ideas, too. He envisioned a future in which computers would become as common and as useful as telephones. Every person would have at least one. At the time, this was considered a wild idea. However, Jobs firmly believed in his vision, and he had a plan to achieve it.

He was convinced that if Apple could build fully assembled, easy-to-use computers, the company would change the world. Jobs explained:

> *The Apple I took us over a big hurdle, but a lot of people who wanted to use the product were unable to. We were getting some feedback from a fairly small sample—maybe 40, 50 people. We were hearing from dealers too. They'd say, "I think*

I can sell 10 times more of these if you would just put a case and keyboard around it." That's where a lot of the direction for Apple II came from. If there hadn't been an Apple I, there would not have been an Apple II. The first product solved some of the problems and exposed the remaining ones in a much clearer light. But we were going on common sense ... We were thinking we should build a computer you could just roll out of the box.[37]

The data from an Apple I was stored on cassette tapes such as this one.

A More Professional Look

With this in mind, Jobs insisted that Apple II be self-contained, meaning it would come with a monitor, a case, and a keyboard, and that it would be small, lightweight, quiet, and attractive. He wanted it to look like a household appliance that the average person would feel comfortable using. To this end, he insisted that the computer be housed in a molded plastic case. At the time, plastic was more expensive than metal or wood, but he believed it would make the machine look sleek and modern. Then, he hired industrial designer Jerry Manock to redesign Apple II to fit his vision. He also hired an engineer named Rod Holt to give the computer a lightweight power supply that did not need cooling. This would eliminate the need for a fan, making the machine quieter. Holt's invention became the standard method. Every computer now uses his design, although he rarely gets credit for it. Finally, Jobs hired an advertising firm to come up with the colorful Apple logo, which has become so recognizable. Then, he kept the firm on to launch an advertising campaign for Apple.

Doing all this required more money than Apple had. Jobs went to banks, Atari, and HP looking for an investor. His youth, long hair, and hippie clothes did not instill confidence in the businesspeople he talked with, and he was repeatedly turned down. Finally, he met Mike Markkula. Markkula was a 34-year-old retiree who had made millions of dollars working as a marketing executive for Intel, the computer chip manufacturer. An individualist himself, he was able to look beyond Jobs's appearance. When Jobs told him about Apple II and his vision for the future, Markkula was hooked. He provided Apple with $92,000 in exchange for a third of the company. As part of his role at Apple, Markkula developed a business plan, which was vital to getting the company off the ground.

The final step was getting Woz to quit HP. He worried that Apple would fail, and he also worried about having to be people's boss. After many arguments with friends and family, Woz was finally convinced to go all in when it was agreed that he

The Apple logo has changed colors over the years, but the basic design has stayed the same.

would join the company as an engineer rather than one of the CEOs. The company became a corporation on January 3, 1977.

Apple Goes Public

In order to get Apple II finished in time for the first West Coast Computer Faire in April 1977, Apple added more employees, many of whom worked round the clock. Jobs was a perfectionist and was often hard on them; at one point, he "was furious that the computer cases had arrived with tiny blemishes on them, so he had his handful of employees sand and polish them."[38] However, the machine was worth the effort. It was the first easy-to-use computer ever made. It had color, high-resolution graphics, sound, and a place to attach game paddles. It was also the first computer to have a programming language built into it. For years to come, other computer manufacturers copied it.

The computer was the hit of the fair. While most of the other displays looked like those of hobbyists, with card tables and homemade posters, Apple's display was slick and professional. The display, the advertising, and the marketing that Jobs insisted on, as well as the innovativeness of Apple II, all put the company on the road to success.

In no time, the company received 300 orders for the machine. That was just the beginning. By 1978, Apple was turning a $2 million profit. By 1980, it was making $335 million, had more than 1,000 employees, and was housed in a huge campus in Cupertino, California. When the company went public, which means that shares of the company were sold on the stock exchange, even more money rolled in. Jobs was suddenly worth more than $217 million, making him—at the age of 25—the youngest person in history to make the Fortune 400 list of tycoons.

Much of the Apple's success was due to Jobs. Moritz explained:

[Apple II] was a product of collaboration and blended contributions ... The color, the slots, the way in which the memory could

The Apple II was the first computer in the world that was simple enough for anyone to use.

be expanded … the control of the keyboard … was Wozniak's contribution. Holt had contributed the extremely significant power supply and Jerry Manock the case … But behind them all Jobs was poking, prodding, and pushing and it was he, with his seemingly inexhaustible supply of energy, who became the chief [decision-maker].[39]

A Demanding Employer

One reason for Apple II's success was that Jobs was as concerned about the machine's construction as he was about its appearance. For instance, he insisted that the wires connecting the computer chips on the computer's internal circuit board be perfectly straight, even though nobody saw them. Attention to detail, he believed, showed consumers the company cared, creating a loyal customer base. Throughout his career, Jobs demanded this same attention to detail in all the company's products. Once again, Jobs was right. Apple's customers are extremely loyal.

To make outstanding products, Jobs hired the most talented people he could find. He was often impatient and outspoken with them, though, and was not considerate of their feelings. Although he made a point of publicly praising Apple employees as the best in the world, he also openly criticized and humiliated them, even if they did nothing wrong. He also continued to shower infrequently and walk around barefoot. Some employees loved him, but most found him impossible to work with. "My job is not to be easy on people," he explained. "My job is to make them better."[40] He was so difficult to get along with that Markkula decided to hire his friend Mike Scott as president of the company, mostly to deal with Jobs. Jobs agreed because he was only 22 at the time and did not really know how to run a company, but he found it hard to give up total control and would often pick fights about tiny issues. Many experts agree

Many Apple employees said that Jobs was not a good boss.

that this is not a good way to motivate employees. According to *Wired* magazine, "psychological studies show that abusive bosses reduce productivity, stifle creativity, and cause high rates of absenteeism [calling in sick], company theft, and turnover."[41] Many employees did quit because of the way Jobs treated them. The ones who stayed did so because they felt that Jobs's methods got results. Jonathan Ive, the chief designer at Apple in the 1990s, said, "The ideas that come from me and my team would

Putting Computers in the Classroom

Few schools had computers in 1979. Jobs strongly believed that if every school had at least one computer, it would change students' lives. He proposed that Apple donate a computer to every school in the United States. This would have cost Apple $100 million, which the company could not afford. However, if Apple could donate the computers and take a tax deduction, as was allowed for donations to universities, the cost would be $10 million, which Apple could afford.

In 1982, Jobs enlisted the aid of California congressman Pete Stark. He and Jobs drafted the "Kids Can't Wait" bill, which made donations of equipment to K–12 schools tax deductible. Jobs spent two weeks in Washington lobbying for the bill.

Unfortunately, the bill never reached the Senate floor. However, the state of California thought the bill was a good idea and passed a similar bill that covered the state. As a result, Apple donated one computer to every school in California. It donated software and provided free training for teachers. Jobs said that getting computers into the hands of children in this way is one of his greatest accomplishments.

have been completely irrelevant, nowhere, if Steve hadn't been here to push us, work with us, and drive through all the resistance to turn our ideas into products."[42]

Problems at Home

Those early days at Apple were some of the happiest in Jobs's career. However, things were not going as well in his personal life. Jobs was sharing a house with Chrisann Brennan, his high school girlfriend, in 1977, but he was more interested in Apple than in their relationship. When she became pregnant, he refused to speak to her. On May 17, 1978, Brennan gave birth to a baby girl, whom she named Lisa. Brennan said Jobs was the father. He helped name the baby, but for the next two years, he denied she was his and refused to pay child support.

In 1980, Brennan took Jobs to court. He took a paternity test that said Lisa was his child, but he insisted that the test was not enough proof. He was forced to pay child support, but he still refused to see his daughter for several years. Eventually, he came to acknowledge and love Lisa, and her last name was changed to Brennan-Jobs when she was nine years old. He later said, "I wish I had handled it differently. I could not see myself as a father then, so I didn't face up to it."[43] Instead, he continued focusing all his attention on his other baby, Apple.

Chapter **Four**

Beyond Apple

Jobs continued to make Apple grow, and the products the company created forever changed the way society works. Compared to the computers of today, they seem old-fashioned and slow, but at the time there was nothing else like them in the world. Jobs believed wholeheartedly in his vision, and his "reality distortion field" made everyone around him believe in it, too.

However, he was still often cruel to people. He ended his friendship with Daniel Kottke, his best friend from college and one of the people who helped create Apple, by refusing to give him stock options. This meant Kottke did not get a share of Apple's profits. Jobs's desire for control also led to some big mistakes. When the Apple III was created, Jobs tried to take over the project himself without Woz's help; he wanted to be seen as a creator, not Woz's assistant. Unfortunately, he did not have Woz's talent and refused to listen to anyone else's advice, so the computer did not turn out well and few people wanted to buy it. He abandoned the project and tried to come up with something better. His second try was a computer called Lisa. He denied at the time that it was named after his daughter, but in later years, he admitted that it was.

In 1981, even before Lisa hit the market, Jobs turned his

attention to another new computer, the Macintosh (Mac), a low-priced, user-friendly machine, invented by Apple engineer Jef Raskin. It meshed perfectly with Jobs's vision of the future. The Macintosh was a computer for the average person. Jobs insisted that it would change the world.

Taking the Credit

With his private life in disorder, Jobs moved out of the house he shared with Chrisann Brennan and bought an old mansion in Los Gatos, California. He bought very little furniture for it and slept on a mattress on the floor. However, he did not spend much time in the house. His real home was Apple. To help with financing, he got the office-machine company Xerox to invest $1 million in Apple.

A visit to Xerox PARC, the company's research center, provided Jobs with inspiration. He saw a demonstration of a revolutionary computer named Alto that Xerox was working on. It had a point and click graphic user interface, meaning that it had a mouse and could display pictures.

Until then, it was necessary to type in complicated commands to direct the computer. The point and click graphic user interface allowed users to make selections by moving a pointer to onscreen items, which would open individual windows for different documents and cause onscreen menus to pop up. Although this is standard operating procedure today, it was revolutionary back then. Xerox's designers, however, were not as good as Apple's. Jobs recalled, "When I went to Xerox PARC in 1979, I saw a rudimentary graphical user interface. It wasn't complete. It wasn't quite right. But within 10 minutes, it was obvious that every computer in the world would work this way someday."[44] He was, at that time, not happy with the team working on Lisa or with the computer, which was large and expensive. It was not the type of computer that the average person would buy. After he saw the Xerox computer, he took their ideas but improved on them. He asked engineer Bill Atkinson to make changes that are now

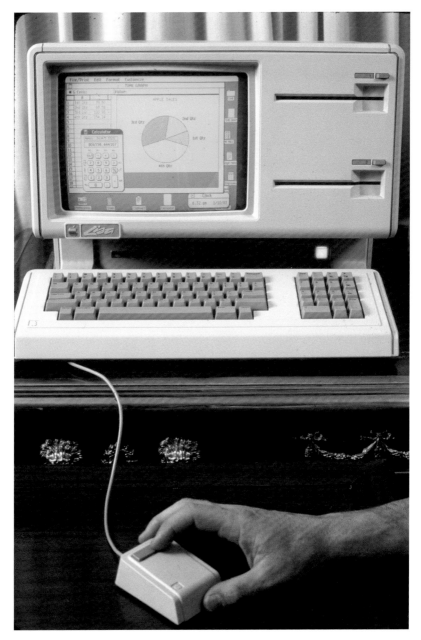

The Lisa was one of the first computers to use pictures and a mouse, but it was too expensive for most people to afford.

Steve Wozniak's Story

Even as a child, Steve Wozniak was an electronics genius. After high school he attended the University of California at Berkeley, where he majored in engineering. However, he preferred actually doing engineering projects to studying about them, so he dropped out in the mid-1970s to work for Hewlett-Packard. He stayed at Hewlett-Packard until he co-founded Apple Computer, Inc. with Steve Jobs.

In 1981, Wozniak was piloting a small airplane, which crashed. He sustained serious injuries. When he recovered, he decided to leave Apple and go back to Berkeley to get his degree. He used the name Rocky Clark so no one would recognize him. At this time, he also formed a corporation called Unite Us in Song (UNUSON), which was dedicated to getting computers into the hands of children, and he sponsored two huge rock concerts, which were nonprofit musical and technological extravaganzas.

Wozniak went back to Apple in 1982. In 1985, he and Jobs won the National Technology Medal. He then left Apple for the final time. Since then, he has funded many charitable projects. He also personally teaches computer skills to schoolchildren.

standard on computers, such as moveable windows and a mouse that moves the cursor in any direction. However, because of his insults to his employees and his demanding attitude, Markkula and Scott told Jobs he could not work on the Lisa project anymore. Lisa ended up not selling well; it was too expensive—$10,000, which would be $28,000 today—and did not have much memory.

A Revolutionary Machine

Because he could no longer work on the Lisa project, Jobs switched his focus to the Macintosh project that engineer Jef Raskin had started. Jobs put many features into the Macintosh that he had put into the Lisa, but he found ways to improve them so the Macintosh would be a better computer.

The Mac team was Apple's elite team, and Jobs let everyone in the company know it. At the same time, Jobs was a strict taskmaster. He routinely stood over team members' shoulders, asking questions and fiddling with their work. When he did not like what he saw, he yelled and criticized until changes were made. He fired team members whose work did not live up to his standards, and it was not unusual for him to take credit for other people's ideas.

Jobs insisted that the Mac be the most technologically advanced computer of its time. He required that it be half the size of other computers and extremely easy to operate. It also had to have a graphic user interface, multiple fonts, sound, drawing and painting capabilities, and a mouse. Such a machine had never been built before.

However, Jobs's team was the best around, and he expected the impossible from them. He convinced his team that they were capable of building it. More than that—he made them believe that they were about to change the world. According to Mac team member Trip Hawkins,

> Steve has a power of vision that is almost frightening. When he believes in something, the power of that vision can literally sweep aside any objections, problems, whatever. They just cease to exist. The reason that Apple succeeded is that we really believed in what we are doing. The key thing was that we weren't in it for the money. We were out to change the world.[45]

However, not everyone felt the same way. Raskin and Jobs often clashed, and Jobs tried to show that he was in control by giving orders just because he could. Raskin wrote an angry

memo to Mike Scott, the company president, saying, "He is a dreadful manager ... Jobs regularly misses appointments ... He acts without thinking and with bad judgment ... He does not give credit where due."[46]

A Fall from Grace

The Macintosh entered the market in 1984. Jobs spent more than $1 million advertising it, including a Super Bowl XVIII commercial. At first, sales were remarkable, but then they slowed. Jobs predicted Apple would sell 2 million machines in the first two years, but he was overly optimistic. Industry wide, computer sales were poor, and Apple was feeling the slump.

The company was now a huge, $2 billion corporation with more than 7,000 employees. The Lisa and Macintosh departments had been combined into one, and Jobs fired many of the people who had worked on Lisa because he said they were not good enough to work for Apple. Many people considered this to be cruel because the employees had worked very hard and had done their best on Lisa. Scott had been fired as well, and Markkula and Wozniak had decided to leave the company. Jobs hired John Sculley, the former CEO of Pepsi, to preside over Apple. At first, the two men got along well, with Sculley accepting Jobs's vision of computers as household appliances. However, when Macintosh sales dipped, Jobs became angry and irrational, lashing out at employees more than ever and making increasingly impossible demands. Finally, Sculley told him that he was removing Jobs from the Macintosh project.

Jobs rebelled against this plan. He tried to get the company's board of directors to fire Sculley and make Jobs the CEO. However, this did not happen. The board voted against Jobs, and he lost control of the Macintosh division. Although he was given the title of chairman of product development, he was stripped of any real power. In 1985, his office was moved off the main Apple campus to a building where he rarely came in contact with other Apple employees. Jobs recalled:

> I was asked to move out of my office. They leased a little building across the street from most of the other Apple buildings. I nicknamed it Siberia. So I moved across the street, and I made sure that all of the executive staff had my home phone number ... I wanted to be useful in any way I could ... but none of them ever

A computer 'for the people'
Apple Inc. launched the Macintosh
with a single $1.5 million commercial

6 Apple Macintosh desktop computer,
   preproduction model, 1984
   Based on the Motorola 68000

The Macintosh improved on many of the Lisa's features.

called. So I used to go to work. I'd get there, and I would have one or two phone calls to perform, a little bit of mail to look at. But most of the corporate management reports stopped flowing by my desk. A few people might see my car in the parking lot and come over and commiserate. And I would get depressed and go home in two or three or four hours, really depressed. I did that a few times, and I decided that it was mentally unhealthy. So I just stopped going in.[47]

The NeXT Company

During a conversation with Paul Berg, a biochemist studying gene therapy, Jobs learned that it often took Berg two weeks to run a single test. When he heard this, Jobs got the idea of building a computer in which students and researchers could simulate experiments. From this idea, NeXT, Inc. was born. The company, Jobs proclaimed, would make "a radically new machine that might enable some obscure kid to simulate a multimillion dollar microbiology laboratory on his screen and then find a cure for cancer."[48]

In September 1985, Jobs officially left Apple, taking five members of his Macintosh team with him. He sold all but one share of his stock in the company to fund NeXT. He immediately hired the most gifted engineers he could find. Like his Macintosh team, these engineers also believed that their work would change the world.

Of course, Jobs demanded that everything at NeXT precisely fit his vision. The building that housed the company had to be an architectural masterpiece, and the factory had to be kept spotless. The computer itself had to have revolutionary technology and flawless style.

This demand for perfection cost Jobs $10 million in the first three years. It also slowed down the completion of the computer, which was not released until 1988. Unlike Apple's previous

A Need for Control

The Apple operating system is referred to as "closed," meaning that Apple keeps tight control over it. For example, music can only be put onto iPods through iTunes, and Macs can only use Apple programs. In contrast, Microsoft's system is "open;" anyone can transfer music to his or her friends via Windows Media Player, or any other music program someone cares to download. This is because Jobs wanted to have complete control over how users experienced Apple products. People who like Microsoft are often people who like to customize their devices, which Apple makes it difficult to do.

Jobs also showed this need for control in all aspects of his life. He wanted to make the decisions about all the products and would delay the launch of a movie or device if everything was not exactly the way he wanted it. He would insult his employees and family members, telling them their ideas were terrible, and he would fight with people over very minor things, sometimes crying until he got his way. For example, he fought with Mike Scott about the length of the Apple II warranty. Scott finally gave up when Jobs burst into tears.

computers that housed the monitor and the computer in one unit, the NeXT computer had a separate monitor and tower with groundbreaking multimedia capabilities, such as full motion video, animation, and the ability to record and store voice messages. However, these innovations came at a steep price. The computer cost $6,500, much more than the average college professor or student could afford. Although universities were impressed with the machine, most universities received donated business computers for free, so they were reluctant to purchase Jobs's creation. The computer did not sell, and the company that Jobs thought would be his greatest triumph was losing money.

Computer Animation

At the same time that Jobs was starting up NeXT, he got involved in another business venture. In 1986, he bought shares in the computer graphics division of Star Wars producer George Lucas's film company for $10 million. These shares gave him the power to make business decisions for the company. At the time, the company, which Jobs renamed Pixar, was developing computer-generated imagery, which they hoped would replace

Jobs bought the Pixar animation company, but it was not successful until several years after he bought it.

traditional special effects and hand-drawn animated movies. They had already created a computer and special software for this purpose. The computer was extremely technical and expensive, costing $125,000. When Jobs saw their work, he was awestruck.

Jobs got the idea of producing and selling the Pixar computer. He imagined doctors using it to enhance MRI and X-ray results or to create three-dimensional images of a patient's body. He also imagined ordinary people using it at home for creative projects. He had the company make a cheaper version, but it still cost $30,000, which was too expensive for individuals. However, it did become common in hospitals.

At the same time, Pixar's animation division was losing money at a rapid pace, and it all was coming out of Jobs's pocket. Jobs considered shutting down the animation division of the company. However, he believed that given time to develop, computer animation would change movies. He did not interfere with the company's creative division because he knew very little about computer animation. Instead, he wrote check after check to keep it open. In a few years, he had spent $50 million. In 1988, he funded the production of *Tin Toy*, one of the company's earliest computer animated films, which was an important milestone for Pixar. *Tin Toy* went on to win an Academy Award for the best animated short film, and it became the inspiration for Pixar's first full-length movie, *Toy Story*. However, those successes were still in the future.

Personal Challenges and Successes

Jobs's personal life was also having its ups and downs. In 1986, his mother, Clara Jobs, died of cancer. His father had died years earlier. His mother's death hit Steve hard. He found that working helped him deal with his grief.

At the same time, new people were entering his life. After his mother died, he searched for his birth parents and found Joanne Simpson, his birth mother, and his sister, Mona Simpson, with whom he became quite close. He had accepted his daughter Lisa

Toy Story was the movie that made Pixar famous.

into his life, although he was still sometimes cruel to her and her mother. Brennan explained: "As Lisa got older, we endured more of Steve's [rude] behaviors: from not showing up for prearranged dinner and dance recitals, to being seven hours late from a trip and not calling me to let me know, to … telling Lisa how beautiful [his girlfriend] was, when at the same time he was telling Lisa she herself was not beautiful."[49]

In 1989, Jobs met Laurene Powell at a lecture he gave at Stanford University, where she was a graduate student studying business administration. Jobs was immediately struck by Powell's beauty and made a point of speaking to her. He found that she was as intelligent as she was attractive, and she was a vegetarian, like Jobs. The two hit it off immediately. He proposed in 1990, and she accepted. Then, no plans were made for several months because Jobs second-guessed his decision. They broke up briefly, and he considered asking an old girlfriend to marry him instead, asking all of his friends which girl they thought was prettier. Eventually, he decided on Powell, and she accepted again.

The couple was married in a Buddhist ceremony in Yosemite National Park on March 18, 1991. The wedding was like Jobs, unconventional and informal. The couple's first child, Reed, was born in September 1991. Two daughters followed, Erin in 1995 and Eve in 1998. Jobs had finally become a traditional family man, and he loved it. He could often be seen roller skating with Lisa, playing ball with Reed, or pushing a baby carriage around the home in Palo Alto where the Jobs family lived.

Turning Things Around

Unfortunately, Jobs's businesses were not going as well as his personal life. Pixar and NeXT were losing a combined $60 million a year. To turn things around, Jobs made dramatic changes in both companies. He closed the hardware and sales division of NeXT, turning the business into a software company that concentrated on developing a computer operating system able to compete with Microsoft's newly released Windows, which it did.

At the same time, he sold the computer division of Pixar, but he left the creative computer animation division intact. He believed that someday it would change the motion picture industry. "Pixar's vision was to tell stories—to make real films," he explained. "Our vision was to make the world's first animated feature film—completely computer synthetic, sets, characters, everything."[50]

Jobs married Laurene Powell in 1991.

Until that happened, Pixar was costing Jobs a fortune. After *Tin Toy* won an Academy Award, he got help. In 1991, Jobs managed to convince the Disney corporation to fund, promote, and distribute three full-length Pixar movies, a miraculous act of persuasion considering Pixar was losing so much money.

Four years later, Pixar came out with *Toy Story*. It was a smash hit. As Jobs imagined, its success launched the computer-animation film industry. Taking advantage of the movie's popularity, Jobs took the company's stock public. It was a bold action because the company was not yet turning a profit. However, the public believed in Jobs. The initial price for the stock was $22 per share, but the demand was so great that it rose to $39 per share in just one day. Jobs, who owned 30 million shares, became a billionaire overnight.

A Triumphant Return

In the decade following Jobs's departure, Apple also had its ups and downs. By 1996, the company was losing money. It had also lost its reputation as an unconventional, cutting-edge company. Apple computers no longer showcased an innovative design or the same attention to detail they had been known for.

Sculley had been forced out in 1993. The new CEO, Gil Amelio, thought that Apple computers needed a groundbreaking new operating system. He wanted Apple to buy NeXT to get their operating system. He also wanted to rehire Jobs. He thought bringing Jobs back would excite the public and raise Apple's sales. "I'm not just buying software. I'm buying Steve Jobs,"[51] Amelio said at the time.

Although he rarely talked about it, Jobs still missed Apple. A few months earlier, when Karen Steel, a former Apple employee who had followed Jobs to NeXT, returned to Apple, Jobs wistfully told her: "It must feel like you're going home."[52]

Jobs secretly longed to go back to the company he had started in his garage. He was even more eager to get rid of NeXT, but he was too clever to let Amelio know how he felt.

Driving a hard deal, Jobs got Apple to pay him $377.5 million for NeXT plus 1.5 million shares of Apple stock, which was a very high price for a losing company. As part of the deal, Jobs agreed to return to Apple as an informal advisor while still being involved in Pixar. This happened in December 1996. Steve Jobs was going home.

Chapter **Five**

A Tragic End

Apple had not done well without Jobs. Some of their products were good, but without Jobs's impressive marketing and attention to detail, they did not sell well. Also, other companies, such as Microsoft, were always improving and updating their products, but Apple was putting out Macintoshes that were so similar to one another, many customers couldn't tell the difference between them.

When Jobs came back to the company, he realized that products would sell better if people did not know much about them before they came out. The company still operates this way; no one hears anything about new products until they are officially announced, which makes people very curious and interested in Apple. Even the employees do not know what the company is working on unless they are directly involved, and sometimes they only know about their own part of the project, not what the finished product will be.

Jobs continued to run Apple from 1997 until 2011, when he stepped down as CEO. He wanted to transition to the less-demanding position of chairman, in which he could advise the company but not have as many stressful decisions to make. Unfortunately, he never got that chance.

Reviving the Company

Apple lost $1.6 billion under Gil Amelio. When Jobs saw the mess the company was in, he started campaigning for change. In July 1997, the board of directors fired Amelio and offered Jobs the CEO position. He turned it down but agreed to serve as a board member and unpaid advisor to help hire the next CEO. He said it was because he did not want to stop being CEO of Pixar, but Isaacson believes Jobs didn't know for sure if he could save the company and didn't want to be known as the CEO who made Apple fail. He was hoping to get the company back on track before he committed.

Jobs knew he had to take some radical steps to save Apple. One of the first things he did was make a deal with Microsoft. In exchange for $150 million, all Macintosh computers would use Microsoft's Internet Explorer browser and its Office software. Jobs announced the deal in August 1997 in front of a large audience of Apple supporters at the annual MacWorld Conference and Expo in Boston. This audience booed the announcement.

In the past, Jobs had accused Microsoft of stealing the idea for Windows from Macintosh. Many Apple fans looked at Microsoft as the enemy, and they felt betrayed by Jobs. However, Jobs knew that this was the best way to help Apple financially, and he was right. The value of the company's stock rose 33 percent as a result of his action.

With enough money to keep the company afloat, Jobs turned his attention to Apple's employees and products. He seemed to be everywhere. He spent hours walking around the Apple campus, questioning whomever he met about who they were and what they did. He also held meetings with different groups of employees where he grilled them about the products they were working on. It was up to each employee to convince Jobs that their product had value. On a few occasions, his blunt manner and probing questions reduced employees to tears.

To save Apple, Jobs made a deal with Microsoft so Apple computers could use Internet Explorer.

Through these exchanges, Jobs identified those people with innovative ideas and those he considered dead weight, whom he fired. Once he was satisfied with Apple's staff, he worked directly with the hundreds of employees who remained on staff. Nothing was done without his knowledge. Not even a paper clip was purchased without his okay. Jobs had taken over.

A New Slogan

The next change Jobs made involved advertising. Apple had lost its image as a hip, cutting-edge company. That image, which was in many ways a reflection of Jobs, helped distinguish Apple from other, more traditional computer companies. Many Apple customers thought of themselves as rebels. When the company's outsider image faded, so did this customer base.

Jobs hired an advertising company to resurrect Apple's image.

With Jobs's input, the company came up with the slogan "Think Different," which was printed on top of pictures of original thinkers such as Albert Einstein, John Lennon, and Mahatma Gandhi, to name a few. It was created not only to improve Apple's sales, but also to remind Apple employees what the company had been and what it could be again. In December 1997, Jobs accepted the position of interim, or temporary, CEO, but he did not want to get paid for it. He was more interested in getting Apple back on track than in getting richer. Jobs explained: "I was worth about over a million dollars when I was twenty-three and over ten million dollars when I was twenty-four, and over a hundred million dollars when I was twenty-five and it wasn't that important because I never did it for the money."[53] However, when he became the official CEO in 2000, he accepted 10 million shares of the company's stock, which was worth more than $800 million.

iCloud

One of Jobs's ideas that was not a physical product was the iCloud, which helps users connect all of their devices. This way, someone who takes a picture on his or her phone can see it later on his or her iPad without having to upload it, which makes sharing notes, videos, music, and other media easy. According to Apple's website, it can even be used to find a missing device. Jobs's main focus in all of his products was making sure they were simple and easy to use; the iCloud helped that even more by syncing everything instantly. Other companies were developing their own versions of the iCloud. Jobs was determined to beat them to it in order to keep Apple as the top tech company, and he succeeded. The other companies soon followed with their own versions.

A Computer for the Internet Age

Jobs's changes were working. Five months after he took over the company, it was turning a profit. With Apple heading in the right direction, he turned his attention to the iMac, short for the Internet Macintosh. It was a new computer, which Steve envisioned as an inexpensive, easy-to-set-up-and-use machine that allowed users to access the Internet.

Keeping with the "Think Different" slogan, Jobs wanted the iMac to look different from other computers. The computer, monitor, and speakers were all contained in a clear, oval case with brightly colored trim. It also had a keyboard that lit up. The machine, which debuted in 1998, was an immediate success. By the end of the year, more than 800,000 were sold. Many of the buyers were first-time computer owners who liked the machine's stylish design and the ease with which it fit into their home. Others were former Apple followers, flocking back to the quirky company they once adored.

Taking advantage of the machine's success, Jobs insisted Apple come out with a laptop version of the machine called the iBook a year later. It became the best-selling laptop computer of its time. As a result, Apple's stock rose to record highs.

Changing the Face of Music

Jobs's next step was even more radical. Taking Apple's "Think Different" campaign to heart, he decided to take the company in a completely new direction. It would change the music industry forever.

Jobs always loved music. When he and Wozniak first met, their love of music by Bob Dylan and The Beatles helped bond them. Jobs imagined consumers using their computers as a digital jukebox. There was already software available that could play digital sound files on a computer, but it was complicated to use. Jobs bought the rights to this software and had Apple engineers simplify it so that Apple owners could easily copy songs from CDs onto their computers. Jobs named this program iTunes.

Now that Apple users could store their favorite songs on their computer, Jobs turned his attention to coming up with a portable device that individuals could transfer their music onto and take with them everywhere. The device was named the iPod.

Similar devices known as MP3 players were already available, but they were clumsy, unattractive, difficult to use, and did not hold many songs. As a music lover, Jobs craved a better way to listen to music—so did many members of his Apple team. Therefore, Jobs decided to create it.

Jobs insisted that the iPod have excellent sound, be so simple to use that listeners could access any song they wanted in less than three pushes of a button, and be capable of holding 1,000 songs. In addition, he insisted the device be small and stylish. While it was in development, he constantly checked and rechecked the device for design, sound, and ease of use. He was not satisfied until it fit his specifications. "We did iTunes because we all love music. We made what we thought was the best jukebox in iTunes," he explained. "Then we all wanted to carry our whole music libraries around with us. The team worked really hard and the reason that they worked so hard is because we all wanted one. You know? The first few hundred customers were us."[54]

The iPod was released in October 2001. It turned out to be Apple's best-selling product yet. It also changed the way people listened to music forever. However, Jobs was not finished yet. At the time, many people were downloading music and trading music files via the Internet without paying for them. Such action was not simple, was illegal, and hurt the music industry. Jobs got the idea of setting up an online music store, known as the iTunes Music Store, which would allow consumers to download their favorite songs for $0.99 per tune. It would be inexpensive, legal, simple to do, and give music lovers access to thousands of songs, including new releases.

Jobs was sure that his idea was the way music would be distributed and sold in the future. He explained:

The iPod changed the way people listened to music.

When we created the iTunes Music Store, we did that because we thought it would be great to be able to buy music electronically ... I mean, it just seemed like the writing on the wall, that eventually all music would be distributed electronically. That seemed obvious because why have the cost? The music industry has huge returns. Why have all this overhead when you can just send electrons around easily?[55]

At first, the recording industry, which was used to distributing and selling music in the traditional way, did not agree with him. However, Jobs never had a problem bending others to his will. His persuasiveness and clarity of vision convinced music industry executives and artists that it was a good idea. The iTunes Music Store opened in April 2003. In its first day, 275,000 songs were downloaded. A year later, more than 85 million songs had been downloaded. By 2008, it had become the largest retailer of music in the United States. It permanently changed the way music is sold and distributed. Once again, Jobs's vision of the future seemed to be just what the public wanted.

A Deadly Diagnosis

It looked like Jobs's life could not get any better. He had a wonderful family whom he adored, Pixar was doing well, and he had turned things around at Apple. However, because he was running two companies, his life was very stressful, and he faced many health problems, such as kidney stones and chronic exhaustion.

In 2004, Steve Jobs's seemingly perfect life came crashing down. He was diagnosed with pancreatic cancer, a disease from which 90 percent of patients die within a year. At the time, the doctor told Jobs that the disease was incurable and typically carried a life expectancy of less than one year. Luckily, Jobs had an extremely rare slow-growing form of pancreatic cancer that, in some cases, surgery can cure. At first, Jobs resisted having surgery, believing he could cure the disease by eating a special diet. When that did not work, he had the surgery. Unfortunately, by that time, the cancer had spread. Jobs started treatment in secret, telling everyone that he had been cured.

Giving Pixar Creative Authority

Jobs did not let his coworkers know about his illness at all until after his surgery. A month later, he returned to Apple part-time and put his friend Tim Cook in charge. Cook became chief

Specialized Stores

Apple retail stores are another one of Jobs's successful creations. The stores sell everything Apple makes, giving consumers a convenient place to learn about and try Apple's products.

The first store opened in Virginia in 2001. At the time, there was no other store like it in the world. As of 2016, there are 484 stores located throughout the world. The stores are all stylishly designed. Many have won architectural awards. All contain a Genius Bar, where customers can ask questions, get technical support, and have products repaired.

Newer stores have a studio where customers can get help in all sorts of creative ventures. The stores offer free group workshops and one-on-one training. There are also special programs for children, including Apple Summer Camp, where kids can take free classes in digital photography, movie making, and other subjects.

The stores are extremely popular. New store openings have become big events, drawing crowds of people who often line up outside the store the night before. Usually the first 1,000 customers are given free gifts such as commemorative tee shirts and goodie bags.

This Apple Store in New York City is just one of hundreds in the world.

Jobs created the iPhone because he did not like the cell phones that were available at the time.

operating officer (COO). Under Jobs's guidance, Apple continued creating more innovative devices that Jobs believed the public would love. One of the most inventive was the iPhone, which debuted in 2007. It was a stylish, simple-to-use cell phone that also served as a handheld mini-computer. With it, Jobs reinvented the telephone. With the iPhone came the invention of apps, although only Apple was making them at the time.

Jobs got the idea for the phone because he wanted a phone with more power and versatility. He reasoned that if Apple could install the same operating system on a cell phone as they used on their computers, the phone would have many of the same capabilities as a computer. Because Apple had already worked with miniaturizing technology with the iPod, creating such a device did not seem impossible. The iPhone ultimately became a huge success.

Although Jobs was deeply involved with Apple, he had not forgotten about Pixar. Under Jobs's leadership, the company was producing one blockbuster hit after another. By 2001, Pixar had earned $2.5 billion, making it one of the most successful movie studios of all time.

In 2003, Disney's contract with Pixar ran out. It took years for Jobs to negotiate another contract to his liking. He knew that one of the reasons for Pixar's success was that he had given the company's creative division free reign to work its magic. Jobs refused to accept any deal that limited its creative freedom.

In 2006, Jobs and Disney finally came to an agreement. Jobs sold stock shares of Pixar to Disney. However, the deal did not remove Jobs from Pixar. Instead, it made Jobs the largest shareholder in Disney. Jobs was now the chairman of Disney's board of directors. The deal also put John Lasseter, the head of Pixar's creative division, in charge of both Pixar's and Disney's animation studios, which guaranteed that Pixar's creative team would not lose the freedom to practice their art without interference.

Jobs thought that the deal was not only good for Pixar, but also for Apple. Someday, he predicted, Apple technology would deliver Disney content; and indeed, many people now watch movies on their phones. "We've been talking about a lot of things," he said. "It's going to be a pretty exciting world looking ahead over the next five years."[56]

Working Until the End

From 2004 until 2011, Jobs battled his cancer. His unusual eating habits made it worse because he was not getting enough nutrients to fight the disease. However, just as he believed his diet would eliminate his need to shower, he believed it would cure his cancer. As the cancer spread to his liver, he continued to publicly deny that he was not healthy. He was receiving drugs to fight the cancer, but because he refused a proper diet, his body was not utilizing them well. Even with all of this, he continued to act as CEO, although Tim Cook made the day-to-day decisions.

In 2009, Jobs got a liver transplant, but by that point, the cancer had spread to other places in his body. Despite his failing health, he continued to work and created the iPad, which launched in 2010. People were excited about the iPad because there were very few tablets at that time, and Apple's tablet was the best because of its touchscreen and ease of use. At this time, he also created the App Store. Now, anyone could make an app, but because Jobs liked to be in control, they all had to go through iTunes. Isaacson explained: "The App Store created a new industry overnight. In dorm rooms and garages and at major media companies, entrepreneurs invented new apps."[57] Everyone had the chance to get rich by creating a popular app.

Not long after the iPad appeared, Google created the Android smartphone, which was very similar to an iPhone. Jobs sued Google because he said it had stolen his ideas, even though he became famous for doing the very same thing to Xerox. The lawsuit was settled in 2014. Apple did not get Google to stop making phones.

After his liver transplant, Jobs appeared to be getting well. He focused more on his work and less on his family, but he was able to attend his son's college graduation. He had plans to create digital textbooks for students to read on their iPads and to "create an integrated television set that is completely easy to use. … It would be seamlessly synced with all of your devices and with iCloud,"[58] he told Isaacson. However, in November 2010, his cancer returned, and he took a break from Apple in 2011 to focus on his health. He still refused to eat properly, so he had a hard time fighting the disease once again. He died on October 5, 2011. He was only 56 years old.

Steve Jobs knew that he was not a nice person, but he defended his actions by saying that his attitude created a company that changed the world. He was not a good manager; his arguments and insults caused his employees a lot of stress, and Apple hired other people to deal directly with the staff. However, it is undeniably true that Jobs's ideas caused a technological revolution and changed the way we live our lives in the 21st century. Other companies based their products on his designs, and he was the first person who believed in making an easy-to-use computer for everyday tasks when other companies were still aiming their products at hobbyists and businesses. If Steve Jobs had never made his user-friendly computers, another company might have, but the way they looked and the things they did would probably have been very different—and so would our lives.

Notes

Introduction: An Influential Man

1. David Coursey, "Steve Jobs Was a Jerk, You Shouldn't Be," *Forbes*, October 12, 2011. www.forbes.com/sites/davidcoursey/2011/10/12/ steve-jobs-was-a-jerk-you-shouldnt-be/#50b4bcb22319.

2. Terry Anzur, "Going to High School with Steve Jobs," Terry Anzur Coaching Services, October 6, 2011. www.terryanzur.com/1605/ going-to-high-school-with-steve-jobs/.

3. Jeffrey S. Young and William L. Simon, *iCon: Steve Jobs, the Greatest Second Act in the History of Business*. Hoboken, NJ: John Wiley, 2005, p. 33.

4. Harry McCracken, "20 Ways Apple's Mac Changed Everything (Other Than the Most Obvious Ones)," *TIME*, January 24, 2014. techland.time.com/2014/01/24/mac-thirtieth-anniversary/.

5. Steve Jobs (Commencement Address), "'You've Got to Find What You Love,' Jobs Says," *Stanford Report*, June 14, 2005. news-service.stanford.edu/ news/2005/june15/jobs-061505.html?view=print.

6. Jobs, "'You've Got to Find What You Love,' Jobs Says."

Chapter One: Pranks and Electronics

7. Robert X. Cringely, *Accidental Empires: How the Boys of Silicon Valley Make Their Millions, Battle Foreign Competition, and Still Can't Get a Date.* New York, NY: Harper Collins, 1996, p. 197.

8. Quoted in Smithsonian Institution Oral and Video Histories, "Steve Jobs," April 20, 1995. americanhistory.si.edu/collections/comphist/sj1.html.

9. Quoted in Smithsonian Institution Oral and Video Histories, "Steve Jobs."

10. Quoted in Jeffrey S. Young, *Steve Jobs: The Journey Is the Reward.* New York, NY: Lynx Books, 1988, p. 24.

11. David A. Kaplan, *The Silicon Boys and Their Valley of Dreams.* New York, NY: William Morrow, 1999, p. 83.

12. Quoted in Smithsonian Institution Oral and Video Histories, "Steve Jobs."

13. Young and Simon, *iCon*, p. 12.

14. Quoted in Michael Moritz, *The Little Kingdom: The Private Story of Apple Computer.* New York, NY: William Morrow, 1984, p. 39.

15. Quoted in Young, *Steve Jobs: The Journey Is the Reward*, p. 28.

16. Steve Wozniak and Gina Smith, *iWoz: Computer Geek to Cult Icon: How I Invented the Personal Computer, Co-founded Apple, and Had Fun Doing It.* New York, NY: W.W. Norton, 2006, p. 88.

17. Quoted in Walter Isaacson, *Steve Jobs*. New York, NY: Simon & Schuster, 2011, e-book.

Chapter Two: Spiritual and Technological Experiments

18. Isaacson, *Steve Jobs*.

19. Quoted in Moritz, *The Little Kingdom*, p. 89.

20. Quoted in Young, *Steve Jobs: The Journey Is the Reward,* p. 59.

21. Quoted in Moritz, *The Little Kingdom*, p. 91.

22. Quoted in Young and Simon, *iCon*, p. 22.

23. Jobs, "'You've Got to Find What You Love,' Jobs Says."

24. Steve Wozniak, "Letters—General Questions Answered," Woz.org, March 1, 2000. www.woz.org/letters/general/91.html.

25. Quoted in Young and Simon, *iCon*, p. 23.

26. Quoted in Kaplan, *The Silicon Boys and Their Valley of Dreams*, p. 86.

27. Quoted in Isaacson, *Steve Jobs*.

28. Moritz, *The Little Kingdom*, p. 111.

29. Wozniak and Smith, *iWoz,* p. 157.

30. Wozniak and Smith, *iWoz,* p. 170.

Chapter Three: The Start of an Empire

31. Ryan Schaub, e-mail interview by author, July 29, 2016.

32. Quoted in Isaacson, *Steve Jobs*.

33. Wozniak and Smith, *iWoz*, p. 172.

34. Isaacson, *Steve Jobs*.

35. Quoted in Young, *Steve Jobs: The Journey Is the Reward*, p. 97.

36. Quoted in Moritz, *The Little Kingdom*, p. 138.

37. Quoted in George Gendron, "The Entrepreneur of the Decade: An Interview with Steve Jobs," Inc.com, April 1989. www.inc.com/magazine/19890401/5602.html.

38. Isaacson, *Steve Jobs*.

39. Moritz, *The Little Kingdom*, p. 191.

40. Quoted in Betsy Morris, "Steve Jobs Speaks Out," CNNMoney.com, March 7, 2008. money.cnn.com/galleries/2008/fortune/0803/gallery.jobsqna.fortune/5.html.

41. Ben Austen, "The Story of Steve Jobs: An Inspiration or a Cautionary Tale?" *Wired*, July 23, 2012. www.wired.com/2012/07/ff_stevejobs/.

42. Quoted in Isaacson, *Steve Jobs*.

43. Quoted in Isaacson, *Steve Jobs*.

Chapter Four: Beyond Apple

44. Quoted in Gary Wolf, "Steve Jobs: The NeXT Great Thing," *Wired.* www.wired.com/wired/archive/4.02/jobs_pr.html.

45. Quoted in Young and Simon, *iCon*, p. 62.

46. Quoted in Isaacson, *Steve Jobs*.

47. Quoted in G.C. Lubenow and M. Rogers, "Jobs Talks about His Rise and Fall," *Newsweek*, December 30, 1995, p. 51.

48. Quoted in Alan Deutschman, *The Second Coming of Steve Jobs*. New York, NY: Broadway Books, 2000, p. 46.

49. Chrisann Brennan, *The Bite in the Apple: A Memoir of My Life with Steve Jobs*. New York, NY: St. Martin's Press, 2013, p. 259.

50. Quoted in Young and Simon, *iCon*, p. 160.

51. Quoted in Deutschman, *The Second Coming of Steve Jobs*, p. 237.

52. Quoted in Deutschman, *The Second Coming of Steve Jobs*, p. 236.

Chapter Five: A Tragic End

53. Quoted in PBS, "The Nerds" (The Television Program Transcripts: Part 1), PBS.org. www.pbs.org/nerds/part1.html.

54. Quoted in Betsy Morris, "What Makes Apple

Golden," CNNMoney.com, March 3, 2008. money.
cnn.com/2008/02/29/news/companies/amac_
apple.fortune/index.htm.

55. Quoted in Morris, "What Makes Apple Golden."

56. Quoted in Peter Burrows and Ronald Grover,
"Steve Jobs's Magic Kingdom," *Business Week*,
February 6, 2006. www.businessweek.com/
magazine/content/06_06/b3970001.htm.

57. Isaacson, *Steve Jobs*.

58. Quoted in Isaacson, *Steve Jobs*.

Steve Jobs Year by Year

1955

Steven Paul Jobs is born on February 24, 1955, in San Francisco, California, and adopted by Paul and Clara Jobs.

1960

The Jobs family moves to the Silicon Valley.

1969

Jobs meets Steve Wozniak.

1971

Jobs and Wozniak make and sell illegal blue boxes.

1972

Jobs graduates high school and goes to Reed College.

1973

Jobs drops out of college.

1974

Jobs gets a job at Atari, then goes to India.

1975

Jobs returns to Atari upon his return from India. He reconnects with Wozniak.

1976

Jobs founds Apple with Steve Wozniak.

1978

Jobs's daughter, Lisa Brennan-Jobs, is born.

1979

Jobs sees the work Xerox PARC is doing and incorporates those features into Apple's computers.

1980

Apple Computer, Inc. becomes a publicly traded company. Jobs becomes a millionaire.

1981

Jobs takes charge of Apple's Macintosh division.

1984

The Macintosh debuts.

1985

Jobs loses control of Apple. He starts NeXT.

1986

Jobs buys Pixar.

1989

Jobs meets Laurene Powell.

1991

Jobs marries Laurene Powell. His son Reed is born. He signs a deal between Pixar and Disney, which provides Pixar with financing.

1995

Jobs's daughter Erin is born. *Toy Story* is released, and Pixar becomes a publicly traded company, making Jobs a billionaire.

1996

Apple buys NeXT. Jobs returns to Apple.

1997

Jobs becomes Apple's interim CEO.

1998
Jobs's daughter Eve is born. The iMac debuts.

2000
Jobs becomes the official CEO of Apple.

2001
The iPod debuts.

2003
Jobs is diagnosed with pancreatic cancer. The iTunes Music Store opens.

2004
Jobs undergoes surgery to remove his cancer.

2006
Jobs sells shares of Pixar to Disney. He becomes the chairman of Disney's board of directors.

2007
The iPhone debuts.

2008
The App Store opens on iTunes.

2009
Jobs gets a liver transplant to treat his spreading cancer.

2010
The iPad debuts. Apple sues Google for copyright infringement when Google releases its Android phone.

2011
The iCloud is revealed. Jobs loses his battle with cancer at age 56.

For More Information

Books

Jobs, Steve, and George W. Beahm. *I, Steve: Steve Jobs, in His Own Words*. Chicago, IL: B2 Books, 2011.
This collection of quotes from Steve Jobs features his views on marketing, computers, Apple, and general thoughts about life.

Lemke, Donald B. *Steve Jobs, Steve Wozniak and the Personal Computer*. Mankato, MN: Capstone Press, 2007.
The story of how Steve Jobs and Steve Wozniak started Apple and changed how people use computers is told in a graphic novel format.

McManus, Sean. *How to Code in 10 Easy Lessons: Learn How to Design and Code Your Very Own Computer Game*. Lake Forest, CA: Walter Foster Jr, 2015.
This book teaches young adults how to create their own website or computer game with a step-by-step walkthrough. Information about Scratch software is included.

Phelan, Glen. *Digital Revolution: The Quest to Build Tiny Transistors*. Washington, DC: National Geographic Children's Books, 2006.
This book discusses the history of computing and how people have tried for many years to make computers and other technology smaller, faster, and more accurate. It includes explanations of the part electricity plays in making these machines run.

Wentk, Richard. *Teach Yourself Visually: Raspberry Pi*. Visual, 2014.
This PDF e-book gives information on how to build and program the Raspberry Pi, a modern computer kit that costs between $5 and $35. For kids who are interested in learning about computer programming, this book gives the basics of how to get started and instructions for hands-on projects.

Websites

Black Girls CODE (www.blackgirlscode.com)
This nonprofit organization aims to empower young women of
color by conducting workshops and after-school programs
to teach lessons in computer coding. The goal of Black Girls
CODE is to give young women who have little access to computers or programming lessons the tools to be competitive job
candidates in the technology field.

Codecademy (www.codecademy.com)
Anyone of any age can sign up on this website for free to learn
how to code. The site features interactive lessons in 11 different
programming languages, including Python, Java, and Ruby.

Folklore (www.folklore.org)
A website dedicated to the history of Apple. It offers many interesting first-person accounts from various people involved with
Apple, such as Andy Hertzfeld and Bruce Horn, who worked
on the original Macintosh project.

Girls Who Code (www.girlswhocode.com)
Young women are often discouraged from taking classes in science and technology, and interest in these subjects tends to
decrease between the ages of 13 and 17. Girls Who Code aims
to close the gender gap in these fields by holding after-school
programs and summer camps to make coding fun and interesting for young women and encourage their interest in the field
of technology.

Smithsonian Institute Oral and Video Histories (americanhis-
tory.si.edu/comphist/sj1.html)
This site offers a lengthy interview with Jobs, conducted in 1995.

Woz.org (www.woz.org)
Steve Wozniak's personal website is where he answers fan let-
ters, posts news items, and discusses his relationship with
Steve Jobs.

Index

Picture Credits

About the Author

Sophie Washburne has been a freelance writer and editor of young adult and adult books for more than 10 years. She travels extensively with her husband, Alan. When they are not traveling, they live in Wales with their cat, Zoe. Sophie enjoys doing crafts and cooking when she has spare time. She is happy computer technology led to the creation of laptops so she can write no matter where she is in the world.